AMERICAN ICONS

★★★

The White House

Aaron Carr

LET'S READ

AV²
BY WEIGL™

ADDED VALUE • AUDIO VISUAL

AV² provides enriched content that supplements and complements this book. Weigl's AV² books strive to create inspired learning and engage young minds in a total learning experience.

Your AV² Media Enhanced books come alive with...

Audio
Listen to sections of the book read aloud.

Video
Watch informative video clips.

Embedded Weblinks
Gain additional information for research.

Try This!
Complete activities and hands-on experiments.

Key Words
Study vocabulary, and complete a matching word activity.

Quizzes
Test your knowledge.

Slide Show
View images and captions, and prepare a presentation.

Go to www.av2books.com, and enter this book's unique code.

BOOK CODE

W381521

AV² by Weigl brings you media enhanced books that support active learning.

... and much, much more!

Published by AV² by Weigl
350 5th Avenue, 59th Floor New York, NY 10118
Websites: www.av2books.com www.weigl.com

Library of Congress Control Number: 2013953031

ISBN 978-1-4896-0532-0 (hardcover)
ISBN 978-1-4896-0533-7 (softcover)
ISBN 978-1-4896-0534-4 (single-user eBook)
ISBN 978-1-4896-0535-1 (multi-user eBook)

Printed in the United States of America in North Mankato, Minnesota
1 2 3 4 5 6 7 8 9 0 17 16 15 14 13

122013
WEP301113

Every reasonable effort has been made to trace ownership and to obtain permission to reprint copyright material. The publishers would be pleased to have any errors or omissions brought to their attention so that they may be corrected in subsequent printings.

Weigl acknowledges Getty Images as the primary image supplier for this title.

Project Coordinator: Aaron Carr
Designer: Mandy Christiansen

CONTENTS

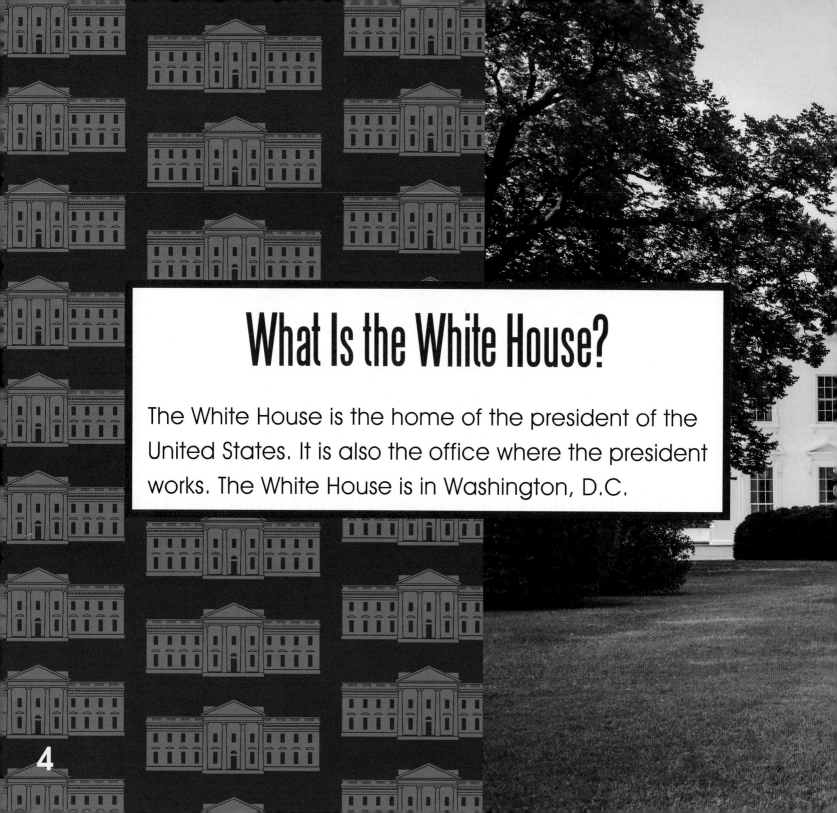

What Is the White House?

The White House is the home of the president of the United States. It is also the office where the president works. The White House is in Washington, D.C.

A National Symbol

The White House is more than 200 years old. Every American president except George Washington lived there. It has become a symbol of the United States and its government.

In Need of a Home

George Washington was the first president of the United States. In 1791, he chose the place where the White House would be built. The same year, the city of Washington, D.C. was founded as the nation's capital.

10

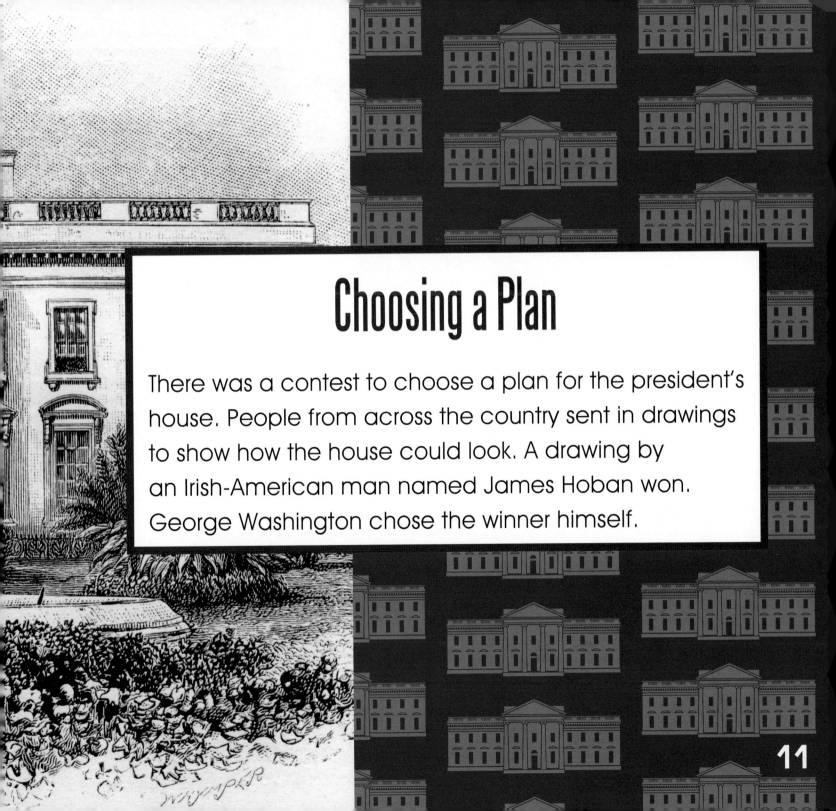

Choosing a Plan

There was a contest to choose a plan for the president's house. People from across the country sent in drawings to show how the house could look. A drawing by an Irish-American man named James Hoban won. George Washington chose the winner himself.

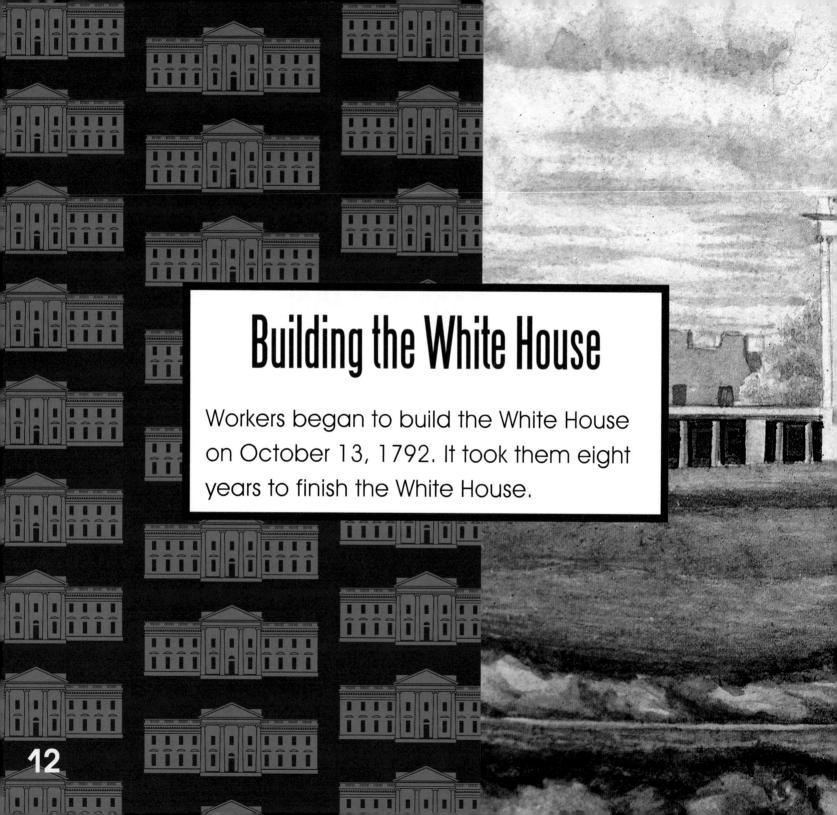

Building the White House

Workers began to build the White House on October 13, 1792. It took them eight years to finish the White House.

13

14

Burned and Rebuilt

The White House burned down during the War of 1812. Only a few parts of the outside walls were left after the fire. It took three years after the fire to rebuild the White House.

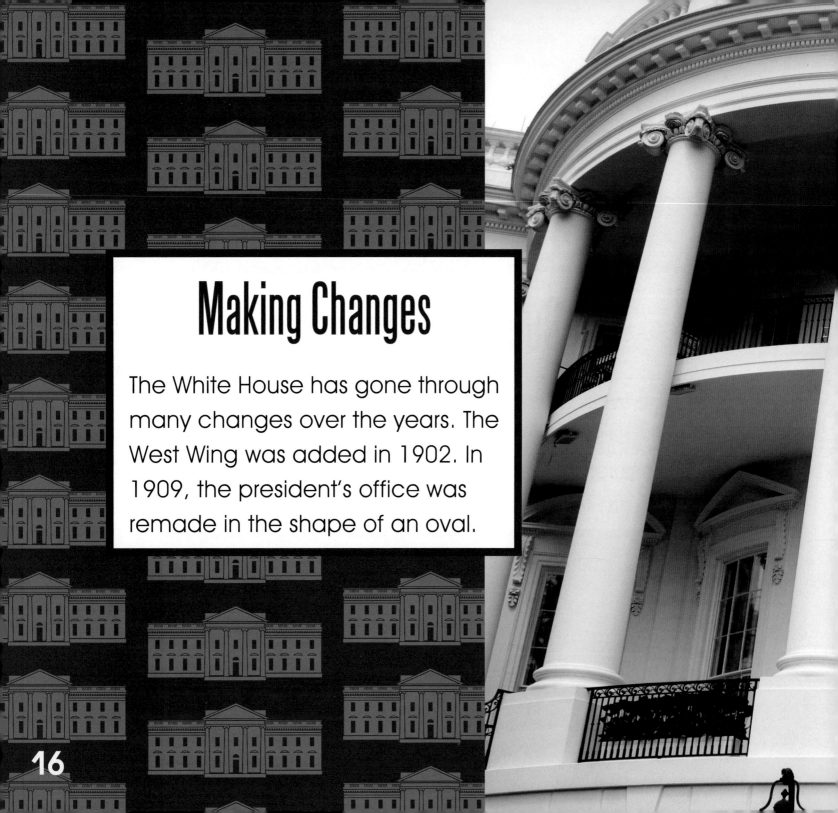

Making Changes

The White House has gone through many changes over the years. The West Wing was added in 1902. In 1909, the president's office was remade in the shape of an oval.

Updates and Repairs

The White House has been kept up to date over the years. Electricity, gas, and telephones were added. The White House had become unsafe by the late 1940s. From 1948 to 1952, the inside of the White House was rebuilt to make it safe.

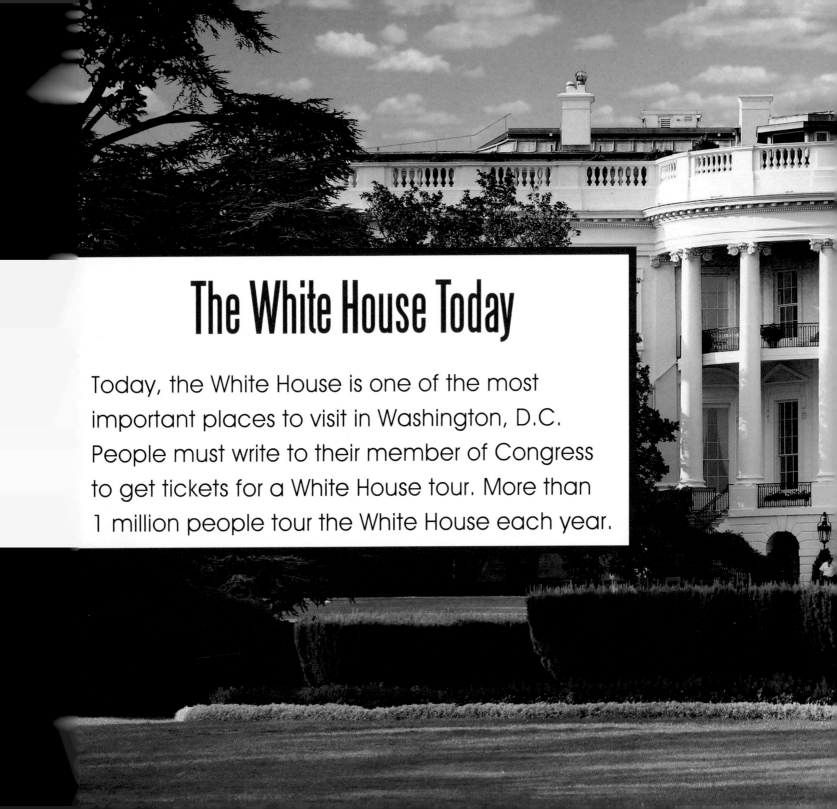

The White House Today

Today, the White House is one of the most important places to visit in Washington, D.C. People must write to their member of Congress to get tickets for a White House tour. More than 1 million people tour the White House each year.

WHITE HOUSE FACTS

These pages provide detailed information that expands on the interesting facts found in the book. These pages are intended to be used by adults to help young readers round out their knowledge of each national symbol featured in the *American Icons* series.

Pages 4–5

What Is the White House? The White House is the home and office of the President of the United States. It is a 132-room, 6-level mansion located at 1600 Pennsylvania Avenue Northwest in Washington, D.C. The main part of the White House is the Executive Residence where the president and his family live. The West Wing has offices for the president and his staff. The East Wing has more offices. This is where the First Lady often has her office.

Pages 6–7

A National Symbol The White House is the oldest federal building in Washington, D.C. President John Adams was the first resident of the White House. He moved in shortly before it was finished in 1800. The White House has since become a symbol of the president, the government, and the country. Though it had been known as the White House for almost 100 years due to its distinctive color, the name did not become official until 1901.

Pages 8–9

In Need of a Home George Washington was sworn in as the first president of the United States on April 30, 1789. At that time, New York was the capital of the United States. Washington lived in two houses there. The capital was moved to Philadelphia in 1790. In 1791, Washington selected the location of the official president's house in an area being developed to serve as the nation's capital. This area later became Washington, D.C.

Pages 10–11

Choosing a Plan A competition was held in 1792 to choose a design for the president's house. Several architects sent in drawings of possible designs for the house. President Washington reviewed about half a dozen drawings and chose one by Irish-born architect James Hoban. One of the drawings not selected was signed "A.Z." Some historians believe this was submitted by one of the founding fathers of the United States, Thomas Jefferson.

Building the White House Construction on the president's house began on October 13, 1792, with the laying of the first cornerstone. The house was to be three stories, made of sandstone from Aquia Creek in Virginia, and set on an 18-acre (7.2-hectare) lot. It took workers eight years to finish construction. Most of the workers were local, but a team of stonemasons from Edinburgh, Scotland, arrived in 1793 to help. Construction was completed in 1800.

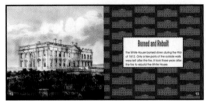

Burned and Rebuilt In 1814, during the War of 1812, British troops captured and burned the White House. President James Madison and his family had to live in another house nearby. James Hoban led the rebuilding of the White House in 1815, but most of the original building had been lost. Hoban changed the design of the White House at this time, adding east and west terraces. The reconstruction was finished in 1817.

Making Changes Hoban also began an expansion project around the same time as the reconstruction. In 1924, the circular South Portico was added, and the columned North Portico was added in 1929. In 1902, President Theodore Roosevelt had the West Wing built to house office space and create more family space in the main part of the house. President Howard Taft renovated the West Wing in 1909, which included making the president's office into an oval shape. The East Wing was added in 1942.

Updates and Repairs In 1948, the White House was found to be unsafe, which resulted in a four-year project to overhaul the interior. The only change to the outside of the building was the addition of a second-floor balcony on the South Portico. The last major change to the White House was made in the 1960s by First Lady Jacqueline Kennedy. She redecorated the rooms of the White House with displays of historic items and art pieces.

The White House Today The White House serves as the home of the president and his family, the workplace of the president and his staff, and a museum of American history. Since President Thomas Jefferson first opened the White House to the public, millions of people have visited and toured the facility. Each year, more than 1 million people visit the White House. All visitors must first apply for a tour through their member of Congress.

KEY WORDS

Research has shown that as much as 65 percent of all written material published in English is made up of 300 words. These 300 words cannot be taught using pictures or learned by sounding them out. They must be recognized by sight. This book contains 74 common sight words to help young readers improve their reading fluency and comprehension. This book also teaches young readers several important content words, such as nouns. These words are paired with pictures to aid in learning and improve understanding.

Page	Sight Words First Appearance
4	also, home, house, in, is, it, of, the, what, where, white, works
7	a, American, and, every, has, its, lived, more, old, than, there, years
8	as, be, city, first, he, need, place, same, was, would
11	an, by, country, for, from, how, look, man, named, people, show, to
12	began, on, them, took
15	after, down, few, left, only, parts, three, were
16	changes, many, over, through
19	been, had, make, up
20	each, get, important, most, must, one, their, write

Page	Content Words First Appearance
4	office, president, United States, Washington, D. C., White House
7	George Washington, government, symbol
8	capital, nation, Philadelphia
11	contest, drawings, James Hoban, plan
12	workers
15	fire, walls, War of 1812
16	oval, shape, West Wing
19	electricity, gas, telephones
20	member of Congress, tickets, tour

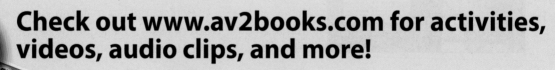